Lincoln
IN OLD PHOTOGRAPHS

Collected by
DAVID CUPPLEDITCH

Budding
BOOKS

A Budding Book

First published in 1993 by Alan Sutton
Publishing Limited

This edition published in 1998 by Budding Books,
an imprint of Sutton Publishing Limited
Phoenix Mill · Thrupp · Stroud · Gloucestershire
GL5 2BU

Copyright © David Cuppleditch, 1993

A catalogue record for this book is available from
the British Library

ISBN 1-84015-047-5

Typesetting and origination by
Sutton Publishing Limited.
Printed in Great Britain by
WBC Limited, Bridgend, Mid-Glamorgan.

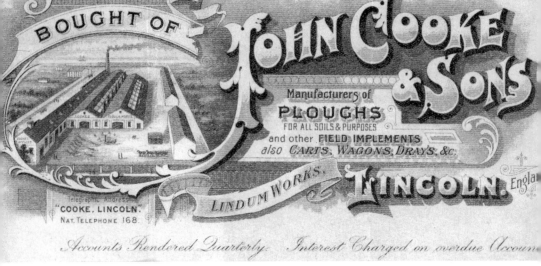

The biggest Lincoln manufacturer of carts, wagons and drays was John Cooke's Lindum
Works. This was their letterheading.

s/08 NA2

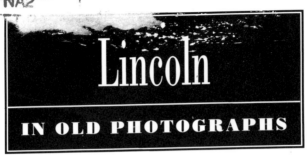

Lincoln

IN OLD PHOTOGRAPHS

In Victorian times water traffic on the Brayford ran at a gentle pace.

Introduction

Compared with Lincoln's long and illustrious history, photography is a relatively new art form, the earliest photographs in this collection dating roughly from the 1860s. The art of photography went on to record fashions, events, buildings and people in a way that the early Victorians never thought possible.

Nineteenth-century Lincoln thrived on industry, producing threshing machines and agricultural equipment. During that time Lincoln's population increased from 7,205 in 1801 to a staggering 41,491 in 1891, which was significant in terms of attracting jobs and employment. In the last hundred years, however, Lincoln's population has only doubled to stand at 84,800 in 1991.

Although the Victorians were an industrious lot, they were also strict and probably slightly hypocritical in their ways. A Victorian Lincoln MP, Colonel Charles Sibthorp, was a constant target for the cartoonists and caricaturists of his day. He once undertook the feat of driving a 'four-in-hand' down the severe gradient of Steep Hill for a wager. After this reckless piece of bravado a handrail was placed half-way up Steep Hill to prevent future generations from trying to emulate him.

The one thing the Victorians did not have to deal with was the unions, at least not seriously. After 1924 Lincoln regularly voted Labour, apart from a spell between 1931 and 1945 when the Conservative Liddall was voted in.

From 1945 to 1979 Lincoln returned Labour MPs. These included Deer, De Frietas, Dick Taverne, and Margaret Jackson (now Margaret Beckett). In 1973 Dick Taverne, who was disillusioned with the then Labour goverment, stood as an Independent (he called it Democratic Labour) and won. His election was an almost unprecedented step, indicating that the people of Lincoln were growing weary of Labour's policies.

Over the years the city of Lincoln has enjoyed the patronage of many of its county's wealthy families: the Waldo-Sibthorps, the Monsons, the Cracroft-Amcotts, the Heneages, the Chaplins, the Nevilles, the Ellisons, and the Leslie-Melvilles. (It always seems to be the same families which crop up throughout history.) Then came the industrialists with their new wealth: the Claytons, Newsums, Shuttleworths and Rustons.

But Lincoln has also experienced some not so wealthy characters, still remembered years after their demise. Their only claim to fame was their individuality. For example, John Banks Smith was known locally as 'Cuckoo' Smith because he sold a comic paper called the *Cuckoo*. Invariably he attracted crowds of small boys and urchins, who all imitated him. Although his jacket and trousers were in a poor state of repair, he still wore a silk topper and it was said that he had been well off at one time, owning his own carriage and pair.

A popular couple were fiddler Joe and his wife, who together would tour the hostelries and pubs of the city; she sang while he scratched at an old violin. Their repertoire was limited in that it only appeared to consist of two ditties 'Down among the Coal' and 'Pop Goes the Weasel'. Another favourite character, who had a bakery shop on Waterside North, was Frank Walker, better known as 'Pie' Walker. Whenever the mood took him he would hawk his hot pies and gravy around the streets of Lincoln, keeping them warm with a coke fire on his barrow and yelling 'Tuppence a pie'.

All these characters together with a very healthy middle class were recorded by Lincoln's photographers, who in the 1860s and '70s included Hardy, Whaley and Draper. By 1894 there were no less than six professional photographers (listed as George Hadley, Charles Moreland, Edward Seaman, William Arthur Skill, Robert Slingsby and Caleb Smith).

In the 1920s and '30s Osbourne took Caleb Smith's old studio and even added further premises in High Street. Josiah Burdall Tuffnell had taken over Horace Dudley's studio, Harrisons took over Slingsby's studio and there were two Smiths, Frederick Smith of No. 7 Portland Street and Sam Smith of No. 36 Steep Hill. Add to this Lance Holtby and W. Frank Gadsby and it becomes apparent that Lincoln had perhaps more than its fair share of photographers.

George Tokarski, Robin Clarke and Roy Mackman photographed Lincoln in the fifties, and that job is carried out today by the likes of Peter Sharp, John Middleton, Richard Johnson, John Gibson, Paul Robertson and Ron Davey – to name but a few. All these photographers, together with many visiting photographers and an army of amateurs, have left a wonderful pictorial record.

Although Queen Victoria never came to Lincoln, every reigning monarch of this century has visited the city at some time or other. It has also played host to a string of celebrities. In the sixties Cliff Richard, the Rolling Stones and the Beatles all played to packed audiences in the city.

Lincoln itself has produced many well-known sons in the music and entertainment world. Steve Race (of 'My Music' fame), Keith Fordyce (the disc jockey of the sixties whose real name is Marriott), Keith Graves (the BBC correspondent for the Middle East), Sir Neville Mariner and the late Basil Boothroyd (long-time literary editor of *Punch*) are just a few.

Military connections have always played a large part in the city's development, especially those enjoyed with the RAF. When T.E. Lawrence wanted to retreat from the limelight, while attending Cranwell as Aircraftsman Ross, he rented rooms above what is now Brown's Pie Shop on Steep Hill. He is reputed to have revised his manuscript of *The Seven Pillars of Wisdom* during his stay in Lincoln.

Guy Gibson of 'Dambusters' fame constantly referred to Lincoln in his book *Enemy Coast Ahead*. His dog, Nigger, was buried at Scampton and Richard Todd, who played Gibson in the film, has visited Lincoln on many occasions. The latest connection is the prestigious Red Arrows, the RAF's crack flying team, now based at Scampton.

The one asset which Lincoln holds above all else is its Cathedral. Dedicated to the Blessed Virgin Mary it is a masterpiece of English Gothic architecture. It prompted John Ruskin, the Victorian art critic, to comment, 'I have always held that the Cathedral of Lincoln is out and out the most precious part of architecture in the British Isles and roughly speaking worth any two other cathedrals we have.'

A carte-de-visite to celebrate the marriage of James Hall to Elizabeth Goy in 1870. The photograph was taken by G. Hardy of No. 1 Norman Place, one of Lincoln's earliest photographers.

Another prolific photographer was Robert Slingsby of No. 168 High Street, formerly of No. 2 Norman Street. This cabinet portrait was of James Goy, dental surgeon and brother of Elizabeth shown in the previous photo.

Caleb C. Smith took over Hardy's photographic studio. Smith came from Boston and divided his time between No. 1 Norman Place, Lincoln, and No. 39 Wide Bargate, Boston. He probably used the steam packet which regularly ran up and down the Witham.

Harrison's photographers took over Robert Slingsby's studio at No. 168 High Street and continued the tradition of commercial photography until 1959. This early carte-de-visite shows the clarity of quality photography which Harrison's maintained throughout.

Miss King, taken by Charles A. Draper of No. 283 High Street, 1879. Sadly Charles's son did not follow in his father's footsteps, turning the studio into a shoe shop instead.

The popularity of photography in Victorian times led to a clutch of photographers springing up all over Lincoln. This photo was taken by F. Whaley of No. 24 Silver Street and shows Clara Hall with a nanny. Ford & Wall took over Whaley's studio and continued the profession.

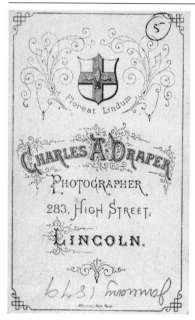

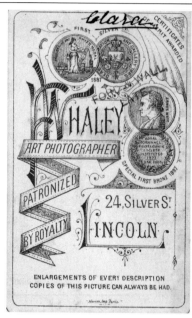

It is often just as interesting to look at the back of these old cartes-de-visite. Left: Draper's advert with his motto 'Floreat Lindum'; right: the back of F. Whaley's carte-de-visite.

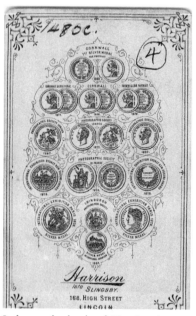

Left: on the back of Harrison's carte-de-visite we see that the firm had also acquired Slingsby's distinguished past medals as well as his goodwill; right: the back of Hadley's carte-de-visite.

A portrait from Hadley's Castle Studio, whose sign was still there a few years ago. Hadley also finished his portraits in oil and watercolour. This was a favourite trick in Victorian times to simulate an original oil painting. By the Edwardian period the technique had become so advanced it was difficult to tell the difference between the two unless the picture was taken out of its frame.

G. HADLEY.   LINCOLN.

CABINET PORTRAIT

JAMES GADSBY   LINCOLN

Another photographer was James Gadsby of No. 45 Sincil Street. This rather faded cabinet portrait of a woman in her wedding dress was taken in 1870. Victorians liked to commemorate their wedding day as something special.

Robert Slingsby's unpretentious and simple portrait of a cleric. Of all these photographers, Slingsby was the most celebrated. He was patronized by his Royal Highness The Prince of Wales and won numerous medals for portraiture.

The Mayor of Lincoln, William Cottingham, in 1878.

The Sheriff of Lincoln, Mr Shepherd,
in 1893.

A delightful cabinet portrait of Victorian ladies, 1870. Slingsby excelled himself when
photographing groups of people.

Joseph Ruston and his wife, Jane, *c.* 1880. The industrialist was one of Lincoln's chief benefactors. The firm of Ruston, Burton and Proctor still survives but has undergone many changes since its foundation in 1857.

Lincoln Drill Hall. It was Ruston's generosity which gave the Lincoln Volunteers a drill hall in 1890. It was built on the site of Newsum's old timber works. Since Ruston's nickname was 'Old Bread and Cheese' the Drill Hall became known as 'Bread and Cheese Hall'.

A Lincoln Volunteer, *c*. 1870.

Lieutenant Gonville Bromhead VC, seen here (extreme right) next to his friend, Lieutenant John Chard VC (seated second from right), was the hero of Rorke's Drift when, in 1879, their small garrison comprising 140 men defended Natal against the might of the Zulu nation. Bromhead was born at Thurlby Hall, just outside Lincoln. He died in 1891.

High Street, Lincoln, 1857. In Bromhead's day Lincoln looked like this, with carts and wagons parked on the side of the cobbled streets. The photo was taken by Henry Edwards.

A Wesleyan family in Grantham Street. Lincoln had its share of amateur photographers as well as the many professional ones mentioned. The note on the back of this photograph reads 'Our Walt 'as taken this with his snapshot'.

Nos 11 and 13 Grantham Street, Lincoln. These slum buildings were demolished in the 1930s.

The Wesleyan Methodist chapel, 'Big Wesley', in Clasketgate. Built in 1836, the chapel was demolished in 1963.

Some of the teachers and children of Rosemary Lane Wesleyan School in the playground. There was a healthy and buoyant Wesleyan community in Victorian Lincoln.

Queen Victoria's Diamond Jubilee, 1897. The crowd that gathered down Lindum Road to watch the procession was enormous. After the repression of Victorian life any excuse to celebrate was a relief.

The Stonebow and High Street were decked with bunting for the Jubilee festivities, and Union Jacks were everywhere. This was before the procession took place.

Even after the Jubilee the same view had the appearance of a decorated Christmas tree.

A large bonfire was built at Branston, as indeed were hundreds across the land, as part of the Jubilee celebrations. The civic party includes Mayor T. Wallis, Miss Wallis, Harold Page and his son (on top of pile with Union Jack) and W.T. Page, Mr Scorer, Mr Oglesby, W.T. Page junior, Mr Lilley, Mr Graham and the Mayoress (on ground or in carriage).

A Victorian Waterside South. The buildings on both sides of the river have been demolished. The area on the left hand side is now the site of the Waterside complex of shops and arcades.

Victorian Lincolnians were an industrious lot. Here we see a group of workmen lowering the level of the road. They then laid cobbles along Minster Yard.

The steps outside the Cathedral were also built at around this time.

When workmen were repaving this area they discovered the drinking well to the right of the photograph, where the old pump can be seen.

In December 1904 typhoid was diagnosed in Lincoln. An epidemic soon followed and lasted until the following May, during which time 131 people died.

Everyone was advised to boil all their drinking water. The cause of the problem was an overflow of effluent from Bracebridge Asylum into the River Witham.

A train bringing in a fresh supply of pure drinking water. An entirely new water supply system eventually solved the problem, when deep bore holes were dug into Elkesley's Nottinghamshire sandstone in 1908.

The typhoid epidemic stretched Lincoln's health care to its limit. An emergency hospital had been hurriedly erected in the Drill Hall in Broadgate.

A patient arriving at the Drill Hall during the epidemic.

A group of people, including many children, collecting water in whatever containers they could lay their hands on. This supply came from Newark, who were quick to provide Lincoln with fresh water.

Mr T. Peel, butcher, was one of the fortunate ones with their own water supply, and he readily helped his neighbours.

Collecting fresh water became an almost daily routine.

The County Hospital coped as best it could. This was Ruston's children's ward, which had been opened in 1892.

The out-patients department at the County Hospital. In 1905 new operating theatres were installed in the hospital and in 1912 a new casualty unit opened.

The old County Hospital. Its imposing frontage had been based on the Hatfield House design by architect Alexander Graham in 1878. In 1914 it boasted 120 beds. The new County Hospital built in 1985 has beds for at least 550 patients.

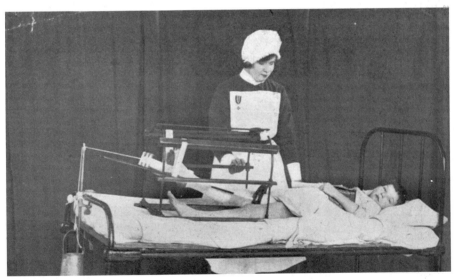

Sister Linum treating a sick child, *c.* 1922.

In Victorian times Lincoln was well known for its annual horse fair, which took place in the last week of April. In *Whitaker's Almanack* it was described as 'The Greatest Fair in England'. Horses stood on both sides of the road, only trotting down the middle of the road when would-be purchasers wanted to see their paces.

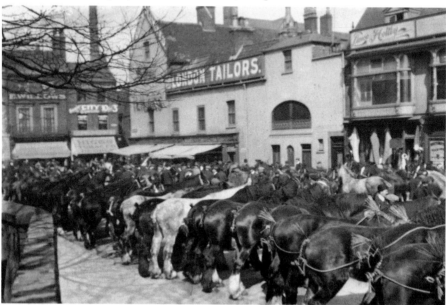

The horse fair also spilled over into St Mary's Street. Gypsy hostlers had a favourite trick of putting ginger around the rear end of the horses to make them appear more lively, alert and high spirited, therefore fetching a higher price.

The West family in a West's taxi, *c.* 1908. With the turn of the century came the advent of the motor car which was to revolutionize travel in the twentieth century.

A group of men on their way to a football match. The group included Messrs J. Belcher, Lloyd, Frear, Brumfield, West, Westerman, Bexley, Hickinbottom, Fox, Brammer and Mills. Charabanc parties were popular as few people could afford the luxury of a car.

Mr George Pimp was the driver of Lincoln's first horse-drawn tram in 1882 and its last, shown here on 22 July 1905. The service 'succumbed to an electric shock after years of faithful service' when in 1905 it was converted to electricity. 'Gone but not forgotten' was the motto.

The opening of the Lincoln electric tramway, 23 November 1905. It had only taken a little over four months to convert the line.

Deliveries from the Great Central Railway station continued to be made by horse-drawn wagon, despite the introduction of electric trams. At the turn of the century Lincoln was served by no less than four different railway companies, one of which was the Great Central.

Mr H. Harrison, the builder, of No. 3 Richmond Grove, Lincoln, shows off his new Minerva motorcycle (34 HP) in 1902.

The Stonebow and Saltergate, *c.* 1889. With the advent of increased traffic the narrow entrance to Saltergate (on the right hand side) eventually had to be widened. The resulting demolition left Pratt & Son (wine merchants) as the corner shop.

Saltergate during the alterations, 1904. The building which latterly had been Lidgetts watch shop has gone.

A fancy dress parade going down Mint Street, with Mawer & Collingham's on the corner. After the death of Queen Victoria in 1901, Edwardian Lincolnians loosened their corsets.

Next to Mawer & Collingham's was H. Beaumont's grocery store and Harston's Music Shop. Beaumont's removed to Silver Street and Harston's was incorporated into Mawer & Collingham's store, making it the most prestigious shop in Lincoln. For the first half of this century few shops could rival its quality or indeed its range of goods. Today it is known as Binns.

King Edward VII, accompanied by the Grand Duke of Hesse and Prince Alfred of Greece, during an official visit to Lincoln on 26 June 1907. J.S. Ruston, the Mayor of Lincoln, welcomed the party and accompanied them to the showground on West Common.

Just about every stage of the King's journey was photographed and recorded.

This photograph of the royal procession was taken by C. Askew.

Lincoln was decorated with flags and bunting for the royal visit. Arches were placed in High Street and Carholme Road with a model of Clayton and Shuttleworth's threshing machine over a sign proclaiming 'Lincoln's Wealth'. This photograph was taken in High Street, with the Queen's Hotel on the left and the church of St Mary le Wigford in the background.

This building was erected on West Common specifically for the Royal Show, which took place from 25–9 June.

Edward VII's visit to the show set a precedent which every other sovereign has followed in the twentieth century.

With the typhoid outbreak clearly imprinted on everyone's mind, the water tower was constructed in Westgate in 1910–11. Eventually Elkesley water was installed into the mains and the Mayor officially turned on the main supply in Lincoln Arboretum in 1911.

A group photograph taken during the Lincoln Triennial Festival in the garden of Dr G.J. Bennett, June 1910. Back row, left to right: Mr Gervase Elwes, Mr Trevitt, Revd C. Scott, J.P. Rayner, Charles Macpherson, Sir Edward Elgar, Francis Harford. Front row: Miss Phyllis Lett, Miss Agnes Nicholls, Miss Carmen Hill, Dr G.J. Bennett. The Lincoln Triennial Festival was held on 8 and 9 June 1910, when four composers, Sir Edward Elgar, Sir Alexander Mackenzie, Mr Granville Bantock and Dr H. Walford Davies, conducted their own works in Lincoln. Elgar conducted his *Dream of Gerontius* in Lincoln Cathedral on 9 June.

When Dr Bennett retired as organist of Lincoln Cathedral he issued copies of this postcard to all his choirboys and choristers.

Another important event of 1910 was the death of Edward King, Bishop of Lincoln (1885–1910). Had Edward King been part of the Roman Catholic Church he would almost certainly have been canonized by now. As it is, people remember Edward King as a devout Christian and benign bishop. In spite of his office he retained the common touch and was greatly respected and loved by all who met him.

Steep Hill, pre–1914, as Edwardian Lincoln basked in peaceful sunshine. It was the golden age of postcards and deltiologists (as we now call them) collected hundreds of cards.

Cornhill, with the Corn Exchange in the background.

Of the many artistic cards, and there were literally hundreds, this one of the Glory Hole, by A.G. Webster, is a fine example. Other artists who sketched the city included 'Jotter' (Walter Hayward Young, 1868–1920), Arthur C. Payne (1856–1933) and Arthur Mackinder. Most of these postcards were produced in The Artist Series and published by J.W. Ruddock of Lincoln.

Ruddock's of Lincoln had purchased Charles Akrill's old established printing, bookselling and stationery business at No. 253 High Street, Lincoln. Charles Akrill, who had further premises in Silver Street, was responsible for producing *Akrill's Visitor's Guide to Lincoln.*

The Grecian Steps, one of the many views captured on postcards. Note the Edwardian lady artist seen through the arch.

The Lion in the Arboretum. Sadly this hapless lion has been the victim of many practical jokes; he was painted with stripes in 1909 and again in 1929.

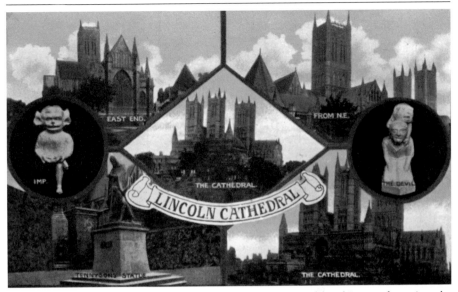

A more common sort of postcard was a composite view, like this one featuring the Lincoln Imp, among various views of the Cathedral and the Tennyson statue.

This painted view of Lincoln from the Brayford, by Arthur C. Payne, seemed to be a favourite. A steamer is clearly visible in the foreground. The card reeks of Edwardian sentimentality.

Joseph Ruston's Monk's Manor (just off Greetwell Road), built in 1870 and demolished in 1932. Lincoln was left with a set of fine large houses, the legacy of the prosperous industry of Victorian and Edwardian England.

'Natty Clayton's Mansion', which stood between Lindum Road and Eastcliffe Road. It was demolished in 1926. Nathaniel Clayton had commissioned Eastcliffe House in 1877 when it was built for between £40,000 and £50,000. Clayton was better known as the other half of Clayton and Shuttleworth.

Boultham Hall, built in 1874 and demolished in 1959. For many years it was the home of Colonel R.G. Ellison. During the First World War it was used as a convalescent home for soldiers, but in 1929 the City Council bought the house and grounds. It was hoped that it might be turned into an old people's home, but nothing came of this scheme and after lying derelict for some years, the building was demolished.

Sudbrooke Holme and its grounds were sold off in 1919 and the area became a residential estate.

Branston Old Hall, which fared better than the aforementioned. Built in 1735, the house was burnt down in 1903 when the occupants were attending a Goose Dinner at the New Hall, then just built. However, it has since been renovated and is now a private house.

Branston Old Hall was the home of the Melville family for many years. In Victorian style, Leslie Melville held a party to celebrate fifty years of marriage.

Lincoln public library. The library was opened by Dr T.E. Page, a distinguished old Lincolnian, on 24 February 1914. The building was made possible by a gift of £10,000 from Andrew Carnegie, the Scottish-American millionaire. Just four months later, on 28 June, Archduke Franz Ferdinand was assassinated in Sarajevo, which precipitated the First World War.

A group of Edwardian ladies chatting casually in Castle Hill Square. They were possibly anxious about the impending war, talk of which had reverberated around Lincoln for months before any official announcement was made.

The Glory Hole, *c.* 1914. The Edwardian era was drawing to a close as war broke out abroad. Perhaps the man in the photograph is contemplating his future.

The Lincolnshire Yeomanry parading in their barracks off Burton Road, as Lincoln quickly mobilized. The barracks are now the home of the Museum of Lincolnshire Life.

Soldiers of the Lincolnshire Yeomanry boarding a train at Lincoln Central station, bound for active service, *c*. 1914.

At home, Lincoln's industrial facilities turned their attention to weapons of war. Foster's machine room proudly boasted 'The Birthplace of the Tanks'.

William Foster's 'Hornet' tank on test for the government on a site off Tritton Road. (Mr W.A. Tritton, managing director of William Foster and Co., was later knighted and the road named after him.)

Women war workers and staff of Foster's in front of their 'Mark 1' tank.

Apart from the 'Hornet' and 'Mark 1', Foster's also made 'Mother' tanks.

Manufacture of the 'Whippet' tank. All these tanks had an enormous impact on the course of the First World War. As Hindenburg, the German general, said, 'We do not fear the English, but when they use their cruel tanks then every possible measure must be employed against these monstrous engines.'

A Robey Short 184 seaplane in the Great Northern Goods Yard, *c.* 1916. The plane was built by Robey's, who helped the war effort by producing aircraft.

Ruston's also made planes for what was then known as the RFC (Royal Flying Corps). This Ruston-built aeroplane was riddled by ack-ack fire, yet still managed to return in one piece.

Largely because of Lincoln's industrial effort, King George V and Queen Mary paid an official visit on 9 April 1918. The King visited the Ruston's Aircraft Works at Boultham.

The royal party outside Clayton and Shuttleworth's factory, which was also on the itinerary.

GUARD OF HONOUR
TO THE KING,
LINCOLN,
APRIL 9TH, 1918.

This was the guard of honour for the King's visit, which also included a presentation of medals and decorations to convalescing soldiers at Lincoln School on the Wragby Road. (The school had been requisitioned as a hospital and convalescent centre.)

The Cattle Market, Lincoln

After the traumas of the First World War, Lincoln looked forward to more peaceful activities. This was the cattle and sheep market off Monks Road. Throughout the inter-war years the cattle market took place on both sides of Monks Road. This site is now occupied by Lincoln College of Technology.

The Lincoln Christmas Fat Stock Show in 1957, shortly before trading ceased altogether. This picture was taken just a bit further up from where Tradex is now situated.

This was Lincoln Ram Sale of 1 August 1919. Back row, left to right: J. Snelson, C. D'a Leaver, A.W.S. Dean, Major Gordon H. Dean DSO, C.S. Fletcher, W. Candy, J.S. Fletcher, J.E.W. Crook, Mr Burton, B. Casswell, T.A. Jackson, A.T. Pears, E.H. Cartwright, C.G. Sharpe, C. Dickinson. Second row: T.M. Cartwright, J.M. Strickland, W.H. Watson, J.H. Dean, E. St. C. Haydon, C. Nicholson, W.A. Richardson, R. Fisher,

W.B. Swallow, -?-, W.H. Rawnsley, -?-, -?-, J. Tomlinson, R. Lamming (sec), E. Shepherd. The people in the front row are unknown. Rams: Champion Ram 'Sturton Lincoln Champion' (left), Reserve Champion Ram 'Moorland 1600 Guineas' (right). (Photograph by Walker of Norman Place.)

A typical view of Exchequergate, *c.* 1930. Note the wonderful old car. Just as Lincoln had enjoyed a brief tourist boom in the Edwardian era, there was also a flurry before the depression.

The firm of A.W. Curtis was formed into a limited company in the 1930s and is one of the few family businesses still operating in Lincoln. It was founded by John Curtis back in 1828, operating from No. 163 High Street. Originally a pork butcher, the firm moved into hams and then bakery. This branch was acquired in the early 1900s.

A group of youngsters eagerly clutching their tickets for a 'Robin' dinner. In the 1920s and '30s 'Robin' dinners were given to those in need, or less fortunate, in the Drill Hall in Broadgate. They were usually held in the New Year.

The Lincoln Corn Exchange, which was above the market in Sincil Street. This was reputedly the site of Lincoln's first cinema. At the close of the day's trading the tellers booths were removed to make way for seating and in the evening picture shows were produced on the screen.

A pavement artist outside the church of St Mary le Wigford, collecting pennies in his cap. There was a marked difference in the twenties between those who had money and those who did not.

The bells of the church of St Mary le Wigford needed attention in the 1920s, which was a specialized job. Over the years the church has required constant repair, a situation compounded nowadays by the amount of traffic that flies past it.

A group of Salvation Army bandsmen collecting monies for the Gresford Colliery Disaster on the site of St Peter at Arches, which was demolished in 1933. In the distance is Mawer & Collingham's and the old Butter Market is propped up behind.

This photograph of the Butter Market must have been taken on a quiet Sunday morning because there is no one about. Part of the façade was eventually incorporated into the Central Market on Waterside South.

A group of workmen leaving Ruston & Proctor Co. on Waterside South.

The Turks Head Hotel, Newport. The depression of the thirties gave rise to bouts of heavy drinking and there was an assortment of pubs and hostelries from which to choose.

The Black Boy Inn in Castle Square, a favourite haunt of bellringers.

Probably the oldest pub was the Harlequin Inn (now a second-hand bookshop), which dates from the fourteenth century. Frank Reynolds was the last landlord before its closure as a pub in 1931.

The Bulls Head at the corner of Silver Street and Clasketgate was demolished in 1957.

Further down Broadgate the Wheatsheaf Inn used to sell Hall's Ely ales. The proprietor, John H. Ashton, also used to organize charabanc parties.

Another pub selling Hall's ales was the Adam and Eve on Lindum Hill. The landlord, Thomas Harrison, dropped a Victorian clanger by hanging a sign outside his pub in 1894 depicting two naked figures. Even though the figures were of Adam and Eve he was forced to remove his sign in the interests of public morality.

The interior of the Adam and Eve had the trappings of a cluttered Victorian parlour. In the twenties and thirties drinking habits had changed. Most people drank beer or ale as opposed to gin, which was a favourite tipple in the nineteenth century. When James Waites, a former proprietor of the Adam and Eve, died in 1813 it was discovered that he had 250 gallons of gin in stock and only a modest 4 gallons of porter.

Despite impoverished times Lincoln still kept its standards. Here sheriff, mayor and other dignitaries lead a civic procession down St Marks Street probably marching to St Mark's church. All these slums have now been demolished and the area is currently the site of Lincoln City bus station.

Clement Attlee addressing the people from the roof of the old Thornbridge Hotel, and restoring a bit of pride into Lincoln's workforce. Just visible is the Witch and Wardrobe pub on Waterside and in the distance the back of the old Liberal Club.

One person who was aware of the changes taking place in Lincoln was Dr G. Morey of No. 1 The Grove (off Nettleham Road). He was a cinematographer who recorded many important developments in the twentieth century. He also kept kangaroos, which caused him some embarrassment when they escaped.

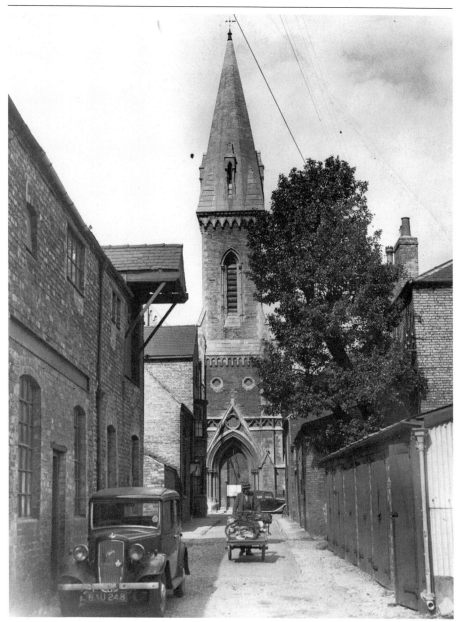

Even in the twenties and thirties traffic congestion was beginning to pose a problem. In the forties and fifties the problems became chronic in several areas, one of which was this narrow street in front of the Newland Reform church. All the buildings in the foreground have now been demolished to make way for road widening and new development.

On 25 Febuary 1922 there was a fire at No. 40 Silver Street which destroyed Curtis & Mawer's furniture shop. Mawer Brothers of Louth (no relation) were given the job of rebuilding the premises; they chose an Edwardian style for their design in spite of the new art deco craze.

One of the more precarious modes of transport were these motor cycles ridden by post office messenger boys. Note the old-fashioned helmets and spats.

The view looking up Broadgate, with an assortment of what would now be termed old vehicles. By the late forties motor cars were becoming more common and traffic signs had to be erected.

After the First World War Ruston's had switched to making motor cars. The trouble was they made them too well; their cars lasted longer, rarely needed repairs and few people came back to buy new ones. Their cars, it would seem, ran forever and 'Quality was the keynote!'

If Ruston's made cars, West's sold them. Here an 1899 Daimler stands beside a more modern version.

Looking up Free School Lane with the Cathedral shrouded in mist. Bicycles are left on the side of the road. Despite the growth of the motor industry, the majority of people still walked or cycled. The buildings beyond the Central Library were pulled down in 1928 when the Lincoln Co-operative Society built a range of new shops.

Between the wars Lincoln was well served by the railway. Apart from Central station there was also Lincoln St Marks. Here we see the roof being demolished in 1957, although the remaining buildings and the line did not close until the mid-1980s.

Lincoln School on Wragby Road was a private school with all the status of a minor public school. Later it became an all boys' grammar school until it amalgamated with the girls' school from Lindum Hill and is now known as Lincoln Christ Hospital School. The impressive frontage was designed by Leonard Stokes, architect, in 1906.

Old boys of Lincoln School include Neville Mariner (now Sir Neville), Basil Boothroyd (long time literary editor of *Punch*) and John Hurt (the actor).

A group of pupils with the headmaster, Patrick Martin, *c.* 1954. The boy eighth from the right looks strangely like a young John Hurt. Patrick Martin left the school in 1962.

There were nine windmills at one time along Lincoln edge (off what is now called Burton Road), overlooking the Trent. This was a post-mill, which in better days had four sails. The only remaining mill is Ellis' mill, which has recently been restored to full working order.

The Prince of Wales (later Edward VIII) leaving the White Hart Hotel with Mayor George Robson in attendance, 25 May 1927. The Prince had visited the city to open the Usher Art Gallery, in the presence of Mr Robson.

No. 7 Lindum Road, a typical Victorian mansion belonging to the Collingham family (of Mawer & Collingham fame). Lincoln Corporation had purchased the house and Temple Gardens. The house was demolished and the Usher Art Gallery was resited within the grounds.

James Ward Usher, a watch and clock dealer who also specialized in jewellery and antique silver, had amassed a fortune from his business at No. 192 High Street. (He also made replicas of the Lincoln Imp.) When he became Sheriff of Lincoln in 1916 Usher promised to leave his valuable collection to the city of his birth. When he died in 1921 he also left a sum of money with which to build a gallery and endow it. Hence the Usher Gallery, designed by Sir Reginald Blomfield.

The old obelisk on High Bridge, which marked the site of St Thomas of Canterbury's chapel, was removed on 15 February 1939.

The girls' high school, half-way up Lindum Road, designed by the Lincoln architect William Watkins in 1893. This red brick and terracotta building is currently the home of Lincoln College of Art.

St Peter at Arches (the tower seen here in the centre of the photo) was removed in 1933 due to the rapidly growing district of St Giles.

It was the Revd A.M. Cook (later sub-dean of Lincoln) who saved St Peter at Arches by suggesting that it should be dismantled stone by stone and rebuilt in the district of St Giles rather than demolished.

Although the ivy is gone, the charming old church of St Benedict's is still there, restored in 1932. In the middle ages it was attended by nearly all of Lincoln's wealthy merchants. The old offices of the *Lincolnshire Echo* can be seen on the left.

Castle Hill House, seen here on the left, was demolished to make way for a municipal car park. The house was purchased by Lincoln Corporation in 1938 for £1,000 from the last owner, Anne Dawson of Newark.

This was the back of the house, viewed from the garden. The house was the residence of Dr J. Stitt-Thomson for many years.

Looking down the Strait with the Jew's House on the right hand side. Originally built when Lincoln had one of the most powerful Jewish communities in England, the Jew's House has fortunately survived the ravages of time. Aaron, a famous Lincoln Jew, financed the building of some forty-five abbeys and manors during the twelfth century. When he died, Henry II had to increase his treasury in order to handle Aaron's estate. Ornaments in Lincoln Cathedral had been pledged to Aaron, who lent money for the building programme.

The sixteenth-century half-timbered building where the Tourist Information Office is now situated was restored by the National Provincial Bank in 1929. Looking through the arch of Exchequergate it makes a glorious composition.

This aerial shot (*c.* 1938) shows the divide between a downhill industrial city with many chimneys and an uphill residential area.

The wall on the right of this photograph has gone, but Pottergate Arch still remains. A road was constructed around the east side in 1938 which left Pottergate Arch as an island in the middle of the road.

The Cathedral from James Street in the 1930s. A charming view that remains virtually unchanged today.

Looking up Bailgate, the business names may have changed but the shops are still there. The firm of Elderkin and the Plough Inn have disappeared, although Mr Elderkin was Mayor of Lincoln in 1931.

Looking down Bailgate, the Lion and Snake public house is still there, but Lyons garage is now a car park.

The age of steam, when fine locomotives like this came flying through Lincoln, has also passed. This photograph was taken when there was a level crossing over High Street at St Marks station.

Looking up Newark Road towards the Cathedral in the 1930s. In this aerial view the gas works are prominent in the foreground, but there have been many changes.

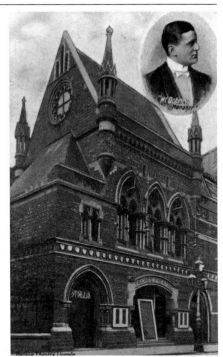

The Palace Theatre, Newland, was built originally as a masonic hall. It then became the Palace Theatre, with Mr Dobney as the manager (see inset), and eventually was turned into the Plaza Cinema. The Plaza was destroyed by fire in 1943.

The row of cottages on the right hand side of St Rumbold Street has been completely demolished, leaving only the Wheatsheaf pub on the corner. These old cottages, cleared as slums, could have been tastefully renovated. Just visible in the distance on the other side of Broadgate is the chapel which is now the City and County Museum.

Lincoln Cathedral, with the Norman House in the foreground, *c.* 1870. The white painted shop belonged to Brummitt (picture frame maker), who was responsible for Brummitt's *Illustrated Guide through Lincoln*. (Photographer unknown.)

Sam Smith's version, taken in the 1920s, differs slightly from the previous photo in the fact that it was taken a bit further up the hill. Sam Smith was responsible for many photographs and postcards, and operated from the Minster Bookshop, Steep Hill, Lincoln.

Lincoln Cathedral from the north-west. This photo was probably taken from the water tower in Westgate. The Victorian church of St-Paul-in-the-Bail in the foreground was demolished in 1971. This version of St-Paul-in-the-Bail was built in 1877, on the site of what was probably the earliest church in Lincolnshire.

The bank of the Witham. In the twenties and thirties river traffic was virtually non-existent, as this photo shows.

Mr Robert Godfrey (Clerk of the Works) alongside the statue of St Hugh on the south-west pinnacle of Lincoln Cathedral. If the opening of the Usher Art Gallery was one great event of the twenties, another great undertaking was the restoration of the Cathedral. The work lasted ten years from 1922 to 1932 after Mr Godfrey had reported the poor state of repair to the Dean and Chapter.

Massive timbers were needed to support the Cathedral while restoration work was in progress. The Constable of the Close and a mason are just visible on the ground and the man half-way up the scaffolding is probably the intrepid Mr Godfrey once again.

This interior view shows the extent the renovation, which cost some £130,000 – no mean sum in the 1920s.

The central tower covered with scaffolding. There were no tubular steel poles readily available in those days, which meant that each wooden piece of scaffolding had to be carefully joined together. The railings in this photo were taken and melted down during the Second World War.

Thomas Charles Fry, Dean of Lincoln from 1910 to 1930. Revd Fry was a remarkable man both as a fund raiser and as a devoted, energetic and resourceful Christian. He made several trips to America, where he raised many thousands of pounds for the building programme.

Bishop William Shuckburgh Swayne (1920–32), who eventually retired to Edinburgh. In his later years he wrote his autobiography entitled *Parson's Pleasure*, a much sought-after tome in Lincoln.

Some of the workmen who helped complete the restoration, 16 August 1932.

Choristers wearing the obligatory starched collars, hats and waistcoats. Doesn't this group look angelic?

Mr Godfrey (once again) standing on the highest point of Lincoln Cathedral, July 1931.

A Robey's compressor had been installed to hose down the stone. The water pressure was so high that it actually cleaned the stone. It is interesting to note that a Lincoln firm should discover the potential of these machines quite so early. Today they are in common use.

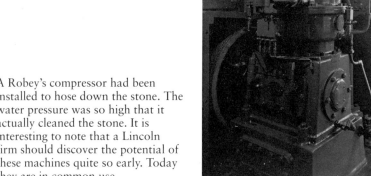

A young Duke and Duchess of York (later King George VI and Queen Elizabeth) attend the service of thanksgiving in the Cathedral, 3 November 1932.

Quite a crowd had gathered to catch a glimpse of the royal couple as they left the Cathedral. On the previous night they had stayed with the Earl of Yarborough.

Bishop Nugent Hicks, formerly Bishop of Gibraltar. Bishop Hicks served from 1933 to 1942, no doubt benefiting from the recent renovations.

Special repairs being carried out in the Angel Choir in 1935. Restoration and repairs were proving to be ongoing problems. Note the *Lincolnshire Echo* van parked at the side of the road.

Mr Straps (on the left) turning out lead for the roof.

The late Walter Toynbee washes down the stonework with a pressure hose.

A particularly good aerial view of Lincoln Cathedral and Castle in pre-Eastgate Hotel days. There have been quite a number of changes since this photograph was taken.

The 1936/7 Burton Road football team, a sport that Lincoln has always enjoyed.

Miss Neville, the first Lady Mayor in Lincoln, in 1925. She is pictured here in the company of Sheriff George John Bennett, outside Mawer & Collingham's.

Ann Speed of Heighington. Ann was quite a character; she could be seen shopping in Lincoln's High Street at the grand old age of 101.

Just outside Lincoln is Heighington, a compact village which had a population of 643 persons in 1891. Autumn threshing was the highlight of the village calendar in Baker's stack yard. As the stacks of corn emptied, Jack Russell dogs waited to catch the rodents that ran from the stacks.

One trade that seems to have died is the old 'smithy'. J.H. Roberts used to have his blacksmith's shop at No. 1 West Parade.

Lincolnshire has long been famous for breeding Lincoln Red Cattle, the Lincoln Curly Coated Pig and Lincolnshire Longwool Sheep. This is the Cartwright family of Grange-de-Lings showing off their Lincolnshire Longwools. The sheep were often dyed but this was purely cosmetic.

The most famous inmate of Lincoln prison was Eamonn De Valera of Sinn Fein, who escaped on 3 February 1919. In this photo the phrase 'It's a fair cop guv' comes readily to mind.

Lincoln prison on Greetwell Road. Built in 1872 by F. Peck, architect, with 'Castellated Gothic and Romanesque touches', the new prison replaced the old Castle Prison, which in Victorian times had become overcrowded.

One of the characters who frequented the city was 'Ratty' Fulton. He was employed by Lincoln Corporation to catch rats for 'tuppence per rat' during Rat Week. He was a familiar character, well known in certain pubs where he could be seen in the company of his dog and ferrets. His contribution cannot be underestimated as Lincoln's rat population, encouraged by waterways, canals and a network of sewers, could easily have become uncontrollable.

'Torksey Ned', a disreputable looking character who wore a battered top hat tied with a string underneath his chin. But it was more than a hat, for underneath it he kept his next meal. He could usually be found on the steps of the Butter Market.

The High Street in the thirties.

One of the more unusual buildings in Lincoln was the Lincoln Savings Bank, appropriately situated in Bank Street.

MOWBRAY & CO., LTD.
GRANTHAM & LINCOLN

BREWERS &
BOTTLERS

WINE, SPIRIT,
AND LIQUEUR
MERCHANTS

15 GUILDHALL
STREET,
LINCOLN

Lincoln also had its own brewers at No. 15 Guildhall Street. Mowbray & Company also had a branch in Grantham.

It is difficult to imagine that this van and this style of architecture were once considered modern. The firm, like the van, no longer exists.

Lincoln Central station during weapons week, 12 November 1940. The Second World War saw Lincoln's industry revert to making weapons once again.

An aerial shot without the vast building programme of post-war Lincoln to the north of the city. Lincoln was bombed during the war and Ruston's was a target for German bombing. However, the factory somehow escaped.

The 40 ft bomb crater in Westwick Gardens, May 1941. The crater was the largest caused by the bombing raid, during which four people lost their lives.

The Home Guard did some sterling service as did the ARP wardens.

George VI visits Lincoln. Photographs of Lincoln during wartime are scarce, and those that do survive are not of exceptionally good quality. The cameraman was perhaps more intent on catching his subject than on the quality of the photograph.

Buglers on the top of the Stonebow for thanksgiving week, 17 April 1944.

VE parties were held on 8 May 1945 when sandwiches and lemonade were doled out to eagerly waiting children. The mood was one of relief that the war was over.

After the war Lincoln tried once again to revert to peaceful activities. The Mayor, Alderman H.W. Martin (Mayor 1949/50), is seated centre of picture at a county Rovers and Rangers conference.

A young looking Duke of Edinburgh visits Lincoln. H.W. Martin is in the entourage.

One of Martin's duties as mayor was to pick the 'bonniest, most beautiful and healthiest of children' for the Welfare Foods service. The scheme provided dried milk, cod liver oil and orange juice to babies and expectant mothers.

GIFT from
FOOD PARCELS
FOR BRITAIN

While there was an emphasis on fitness and health, there were also food shortages. The Mayor, Alderman Martin, is handing out food parcels to the needy, a gift from Pietermaritzburg, South Africa, 22 July 1949. The parcels contained such things as lunch pie, corned beef, dried milk, mixed dried fruit, sausages, lard and tea.

Alderman Martin with the 'Thumb Ring'. This ring is only worn two times during the mayoral year, the first being at the Mayor-making ceremony, and the second when the Mayor visits the city's schools on his official birthday in February. The ring is shown to the children and they are granted one day's holiday. The practice is still continued to this day.

Mayor's officer Mr Leslie Boddy places the great mace on the table in the Guildhall, 1949. This is the position occupied by the mace at all public meetings of the City Council.

Lincoln City Football Club supporters, 1952. Throughout the twenties and thirties the club had attracted quite a following. This was the scene after they had beaten Stockport to gain promotion from Division Three to Division Two.

'What do we do with all our old carriages?' asked British Railways. Well, we can turn one into a classroom. Aware that many of their employees could benefit from further education, this carriage advertised a 'Mutual Improvement Classroom, meetings held every second Sunday in each month, commencing at 2.30 p.m.', as written on the sign affixed to the side of the carriage.

The rear observation coach leaves Lincoln Central station for London in 1953, the year of Queen Elizabeth II's coronation. The coach was made in Lincoln by Claytons.

This early form of three-wheeler or makeshift van is in complete contrast to the stylish railway coach. The front seems to be that of a motor bike, grafted on to a rear chassis of some sort. The whole made something resembling an early Reliant Robin.

Orchard Street Fair in Victorian times. Many famous circuses have also appeared in Lincoln, including Bertram Mills', Billy Smart's, Chipperfield's and, more recently, Gerry Cottle's.

During the Second World War Lincoln's fair moved to the South Common. For many years it had been held on the cattle market on Monks Road and prior to that in Orchard Street. This was the Helter Skelter and Ghost Train being erected in 1955.

Lincoln City Football Club, 6 August 1955. Lincoln were then in Division Two under William 'Bill' Anderson, seen to the right of Door G.

Bill Anderson presenting a cup to the Westgate Boys' team of 1956. Anderson was manager of Lincoln from 1947 to 1965. One of his successors was Graham Taylor, who managed Lincoln in the mid-seventies and who currently manages the England team.

'Hello! Hello! Hello! What's this 'ere then?' This was the Lincoln City Police Force eleven of 1956.

Trying to emulate their heros are members of the Ermine team of 1968, who beat St Peter at Gowts team in the school soccer final.

A group of Lincoln City fans leaving Lincoln Central for Mansfield in 1962. Some City fans were prepared to follow 'The Imps' anywhere.

An action shot of the Lincoln versus Leeds match, 3 March 1956.

City versus Chesterfield, 1963. The stand in the background has since been demolished to make way for a new one.

A queue of supporters hoping to purchase cup tickets at Sincil Bank on 14 December 1963.

The Heighington XI of 1963.

In 1951 Thomas Francis Taylor was Mayor of Lincoln. This photograph of him was taken in St Marks on 3 June 1951, as a military band marched past.

In 1952 the First Battalion of the Royal Lincolnshire Regiment arrived home in England. The first half of the battalion sailed on HT *Empress of Australia* from Port Said. The second half followed in HT *Lancashire*, which docked in Liverpool on 12 May.

It was the first time the regiment had visited the city since 1933. The Mayor, Councillor J.W. Giles, extended a civic welcome in front of the War Memorial in High Street.

He then inspected the troops in the company of the colonel of the regiment, Major General J.A.A. Griffin, and Lt. Colonel Wilson. The Royal Lincolnshire Regiment (10th of Foot) were to be represented in 1953 at the coronation of Queen Elizabeth II by the adjutant of the regiment, Colonel J.L.M. Dymoke (Hereditary Champion of the Queen). The battalion moved to Brooke Barracks, Berlin, in 1954.

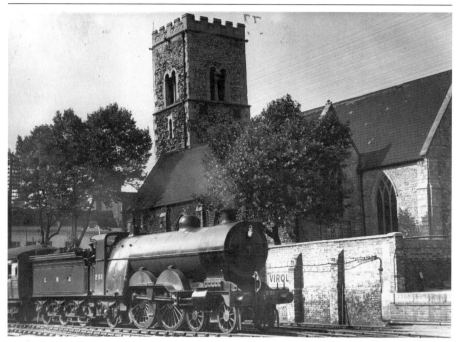

A GNR Large Boiler Atlantic No. 251 railway train, with St Mary le Wigford church in the background, 1954. This type of engine was soon to become a thing of the past as the 1950s saw the change-over from steam to diesel.

In 1964 there was a serious accident when the driver of a Humber Warehousing lorry mistakenly thought he could drive underneath Newport Arch. The only Roman gateway left in England which is still in use could not escape the problems of the twentieth century.

The instruction diesel train brought to Lincoln by British Railways in 1957 to illustrate the advantages of the change-over.

An American articulated lorry in collision with a van at the northern entrance to the Stonebow, 2 July 1952. The problems of increased road traffic were certainly giving the authorities a real headache.

Pelham Bridge shortly after completion. The construction of the bridge was perhaps one of the more drastic road developments to take place in the 1950s.

Her Majesty Queen Elizabeth II and Prince Philip leaving the Judgement Porch of Lincoln Cathedral in the company of Bishop Dunlop (then Dean of Lincoln) and Bishop Riches (Bishop of Lincoln), 27 June 1958. The royal couple had visited the city to open Pelham Bridge.

The Queen quickly inspects the troops meeting her outside Central station on her arrival on 27 June 1958. What is perhaps more fascinating about this photograph, however, is the old Albion Hotel in the background.

There is no doubt that Pelham Bridge eased traffic congestion. However, it posed two further problems. The roundabout in the foreground of this picture would have to go and a foot-bridge would have to be erected over this heavily congested area.

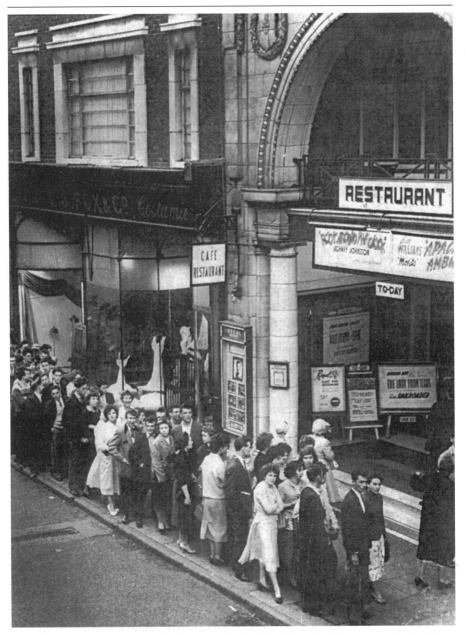

Crowds queuing up to see *Rock Around the Clock* in the fifties outside the Regal Cinema in High Street. The Regal was demolished in the 1960s and today the site forms part of the Littlewoods store.

Of the strange fashions in the fifties suede jackets were the 'in' thing for women. In 1952 Mawer & Collingham's were advertising these jackets at 12 guineas!

This was the men's department of Mawer & Collingham's in 1952. Men's fashions seem to have changed little, apart from the preponderance of headgear.

The Glory Hole. One photographer who did much to promote Lincoln in the post-war years was Hugh Martineau of Woodhall Spa. A schoolmaster by profession and an amateur photographer by choice he recorded and wrote much about Lincoln, especially for *Lincolnshire Life*.

In the early 1960s a film crew and a group of little known actors and actresses descended on Lincoln to film *The Wild and the Willing* – a tale of University life. They included Ian McShane (better known as Lovejoy) (centre) Samantha Eggar, Johnny Briggs (who went on to star in Coronation Street) and John Standing.

Lincoln Cathedral's Christingle service, which featured on London Weekend Television on 1 December 1973.

Simon Phipps, the Bishop of Lincoln, meets Herbert Howells, the composer, in 1975. Bishop Phipps held office from 1975 to 1986.

Mayor Charles Albert Lillicrap giving his Christmas message to the people of Lincoln from the steps of the Cathedral in 1956. In attendance were Bishop Dunlop (Dean), Gordon Slater, Mr Brailsford, Kenneth Riches (Bishop of Lincoln), the Venerable Lisle Marsden (Archdeacon of Lindsey), Cecil Jollands (Lay Sacrist), Mrs Lillicrap (Mayoress), Bishop Arthur Greaves (Precentor).

The cloisters of Lincoln Cathedral, one of the most peaceful spots in Lincoln.

Dr Gordon Slater conducting in the
Cathedral.

Sir John Barbirolli (1899–1970) gave his last public performance in Lincoln Cathedral.

Yehudi Menuhin was just one of the famous names to appear in Lincoln Cathedral in the 1970s. Another was Sir Adrian Boult.

As well as orchestral concerts Lincoln is also the scene of more peaceful rural activities. The traction engine is *Sylvie* (normally housed in the Museum of Lincolnshire Life). Pictured with *Sylvie* are Dorothy and George Moss, Harry Benton and Leslie Colsell. The photo was probably taken at Stragglethorpe.

One event which was extremely popular in post-war Lincoln was the half marathon. It ran for ten years.

Here are a few of the competitors racing down Bailgate.

There was even a disabled section.

The Lincoln Grand Prix, *c*. 1981/2, was another popular event, which was also televised.

Queen Elizabeth signing the visitors' book in Lincoln Cathedral in 1980. The Queen's visit to the city was part of the celebrations of the 700th anniversary of the consecration of the Angel Choir. Also present are Oliver Twisleton Wickham Fiennes (the Dean of Lincoln from 1969 to 1989 and uncle of Sir Ranulph Fiennes, the Arctic explorer), Simon Phipps (the Bishop of Lincoln), Derek Wellman (the Bishop's Registrar) and Cecil Jollands (Chapter Clerk).

Air Vice-Marshal John Brownlow (Commandant of RAF Cranwell) and the Chapter Clerk, Cecil Jollands, partake in a twelve hour sponsored ten pin bowling marathon in aid of Lincoln Cathedral Fabric Fund in July 1980.

The late 'Jack', Earl of Yarborough (centre of photo), donates chestnut wood from his estate at Brocklesby for the Cathedral roof.

The Lawn, 1982. 'The Lawn' Hospital was opened in 1820 and originally known as the Lincoln Asylum, Spring Hill. It was renamed The Lawn in 1884 to overcome the stigma associated with the word 'asylum'. This photograph was taken before the renovations carried out in the late 1980s.

An interior view of The Lawn. One evening in 1985 the Leader of the City Council, Councillor Derek Miller, suggested to the Chief Executive, Mr Thomas, that Lincoln City Council should buy The Lawn. Mr Thomas, it must be said, nearly fainted at the idea. It was agreed, however, and Mr A.J. Tindall purchased the property for £425,000 from the North Lincolnshire Health Authority. The Simons group were given the job of renovation at a cost of £2.5 million. The result is spectacular.

A group of musketeers firing a volley in front of the old Assize Court building in the grounds of Lincoln Castle. In recent times the Castle has been a venue for jousts, sword fighting and archery.

Some of the costumes can be very spectacular.

Lincoln has always maintained a good relationship with the RAF. On 25 April 1959, RAF Waddington was awarded the Freedom of the City of Lincoln, and on 14 May 1993 RAF Scampton was awarded the same honour.

Lincoln City Council, 1991. Back row, left to right: Councillor N. Haigh, Councillor J. O'Brien, Councillor R.S. Hall, Councillor F.H. Martin, Councillor A.R. Toofany (Mayor), Councillor T.P. Rook, Councillor G. Ellis, Councillor A.C. Morgan, Mr P.S. Wright, Mr N.K. Walker, Mr A.R. Rushton, Mr J. Bibby, Mr R.M. Shardlow. Second row: Councillor L.W. Richardson, Councillor E. Noble, Mr P. Hurst, Councillor Mrs N. Baldock, Councillor J.S. Robertson, Councillor R. Hurst, Mr G. Wade, Mr C.J. Thomas, Councillor D.W. Miller, Councillor L.A. Vaisey, Councillor P.J. West, Councillor S.J. Paterson, Mr K.J. Laidler. Front row: Councillor F.R. Robinson, Councillor W. Crumblehulme, Councillor A.K. Bradley, Councillor E.W. Strengiel, Councillor Ms L.K. Woolley, Councillor Mrs B.K. Freeborough, Councillor H. Bunnage, Councillor N.M. Murray, Councillor R.J.A. Metcalfe, Councillor L.C. Wells.

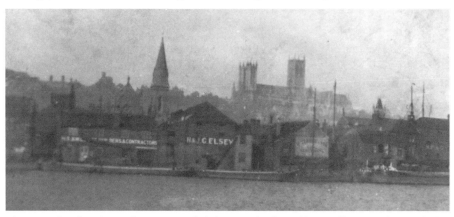

The once familiar firms that surrounded the Brayford Pool have all gone. They included H. & J.G. Elsey, W. Clarke & Son (coal merchants), G. Harrison & Son (corn, cake and hay merchants), Goole Tillage Co. Ltd, C.H. Pacy (corn and coal merchant), J.T. Forrington (corn merchants), H.S. & W. Close (builders and contractors) and Dawson & Co. (maltsters).

The Brayford, *c.* 1970. A new word came into being – 'Simonization', after the Lincoln firm of builders.

Prince Charles walks down the High Street during his visit to Lincoln on 6 July 1979. Crowds of well-wishers look on. Councillor Trevor Rook (the Mayor) is accompanying him. The purpose of the Prince's visit was to look at the restoration work being carried out in the Cathedral and to visit the firm of Ruston-Bucyrus.

Prince Charles returns to Lincoln to open The Lawn on 20 November 1990. The author can be seen talking to the Prince in the company of the Mayor of Lincoln, Councillor D.B. Jackson.

A group of Victorian workmen reinforcing the sides of the canal at Waterside North. Barges bumping up and down the narrow waterway had meant that repairs were necessary. The weight of the obelisk on High Bridge in the background meant that timber supports had to be erected while renovations were carried out.

Acknowledgements

I am particularly grateful to Cliff Smith of the *Lincolnshire Echo* for allowing me to reproduce certain photographs from the *Lincolnshire Echo* archives and Peter Brown of the 'Gossiper' column for relevant information. Special thanks also go to Cecil Jollands, whose memory is as crisp as his sense of humour. Last but not least thanks to Andrea Martin of the Museum of Lincolnshire Life, whose foresight and observation pointed me in the right direction. People who have lent photographs or given permission for the use of their copyright include:

Peter Brown • Neil Curtis • Dean and Chapter • Julie Duxbury • David Elliott
George Exley • Rowland Hall • Cecil Jollands • James and Ann Laverack
Lincoln City Archives • Lincoln City Council • Lincolnshire County Council
Lincolnshire Echo • Andrea Martin • Richard Mawer • the late Fred Morton
C.V. Middleton and Son • Museum of Lincolnshire Life • Geoffrey Roe
Peter Sharp • Charles Smith • Cliff Smith • Wellholme Galleries

I should also like to thank my wife, Sylvia, for typing this manuscript and who can now reclaim the kitchen table.